The Case for India

Annie Besant

ESPRIOS DIGITAL PUBLISHING

THE CASE FOR INDIA

THE PRESIDENTIAL
ADDRESS DELIVERED BY
ANNIE BESANT AT THE
THIRTY-SECOND INDIAN
NATIONAL CONGRESS
HELD AT CALCUTTA
26TH DECEMBER 1917

Presidential Address

Fellow-delegates and friends,

Everyone who has preceded me in this Chair has rendered his thanks in fitting terms for the gift which is truly said to be the highest that India has it in her power to bestow. It is the sign of her fullest love, trust, and approval, and the one whom she seats in that chair is, for his year of service, her chosen leader. But if my predecessors found fitting words for their gratitude, in what words can I voice mine, whose debt to you is so overwhelmingly greater than theirs? For the first time in Congress history, you have chosen as your President one who, when your choice was made, was under the heavy ban of Government displeasure, and who lay interned as a person dangerous to public safety. While I was humiliated, you crowned me with honour; while I was slandered, you believed in my integrity and good faith; while I was crushed under the heel of bureaucratic power, you acclaimed me as your leader; while I was silenced and unable to defend myself, you defended me, and won for me release. I was proud to serve in lowliest fashion, but you lifted me up and placed me before the world as your chosen representative. I have no words with which to thank you, no eloquence with which to repay my debt. My deeds must speak for me, for words are too poor. I turn your gift into service to the Motherland; I consecrate my life anew to her in worship by action. All that I have and am, I lay on the Altar of the Mother, and together we shall cry, more by service than by words: VANDE MATARAM.

There is, perhaps, one value in your election of me in this crisis of India's destiny, seeing that I have not the privilege to be Indian-born, but come from that little island in the northern seas which has been, in the West, the builder-up of free institutions. The Aryan emigrants, who spread over the lands of Europe, carried with them the seeds of liberty sown in their blood in their Asian cradle-land. Western historians trace the self-rule of the Saxon villages to their earlier prototypes in the East, and see the growth of English liberty as up-springing from the Aryan root of the free and self-contained village communities.

Its growth was crippled by Norman feudalism there, as its millennia-nourished security here was smothered by the East India Company. But in England it burst its shackles and nurtured a liberty-loving people and a free Commons' House. Here, it similarly bourgeoned out into the Congress activities, and more recently into those of the Muslim League, now together blossoming into Home Rule for India. The England of Milton, Cromwell, Sydney, Burke, Paine, Shelley, Wilberforce, Gladstone; the England that sheltered Mazzini, Kossuth, Kropotkin, Stepniak, and that welcomed Garibaldi; the England that is the enemy of tyranny, the foe of autocracy, the lover of freedom, that is the England I would fain here represent to you to-day. To-day, when India stands erect, no suppliant people, but a Nation, self-conscious, self-respecting, determined to be free; when she stretches out her hand to Britain and offers friendship not subservience; co-operation not obedience; to-day let me: western-born but in spirit eastern, cradled in England but Indian by choice and adoption: let me stand as the symbol of union between Great Britain and India: a union of hearts and free choice, not of compulsion: and therefore of a tie which cannot be broken, a tie of love and of mutual helpfulness, beneficial to both Nations and blessed by God.

GONE TO THE PEACE.

India's great leader, Dadabhai Naoroji, has left his mortal body and is now one of the company of the Immortals, who watch over and aid India's progress. He is with V.C. Bonnerjee, and Ranade, and A.O. Hume, and Henry Cotton, and Pherozeshah Mehta, and Gopal Krishna Gokhale: the great men who, in Swinburne's noble verse, are the stars which lead us to Liberty's altar:

These, O men, shall ye honour, Liberty only and these. For thy sake and for all men's and mine, Brother, the crowns of them shine, Lighting the way to her shrine, That our eyes may be fastened upon her, That our hands may encompass her knees.

Not for me to praise him in feeble words of reverence or of homage. His deeds praise him, and his service to his country is his abiding glory. Our gratitude will be best paid by following in his footsteps, alike in his splendid courage and his unfaltering devotion, so that we may win the Home Rule which he longed to see while with us, and shall see, ere long, from the other world of Life, in which he dwells today.

CHAPTER I.

PRE-WAR MILITARY EXPENDITURE.

The Great War, into the whirlpool of which Nation after Nation has been drawn, has entered on its fourth year. The rigid censorship which has been established makes it impossible for any outside the circle of Governments to forecast its duration, but to me, speaking for a moment not as a politician but as a student of spiritual laws, to me its end is sure. For the true object of this War is to prove the evil of, and to destroy, autocracy and the enslavement of one Nation by another, and to place on sure foundations the God-given Right to Self-Rule and Self-Development of every Nation, and the similar right of the Individual, of the smaller Self, so far as is consistent with the welfare of the larger Self of the Nation. The forces which make for the prolongation of autocracy—the rule of one—and the even deadlier bureaucracy—the rule of a close body welded into an iron system—these have been gathered together in the Central Powers of Europe—as of old in Ravana—in order that they may be destroyed; for the New Age cannot be opened until the Old passes away. The new civilisation of Righteousness and Justice, and therefore of Brotherhood, of ordered Liberty, of Peace, of Happiness, cannot be built up until the elements are removed which have brought the old civilisation crashing about our ears. Therefore is it necessary that the War shall be fought out to its appointed end, and that no premature peace shall leave its object unattained. Autocracy and bureaucracy must perish utterly, in East and West, and, in order that their germs may not re-sprout in the future, they must be discredited in the minds of men. They must be proved to be less efficient than the Governments of Free Peoples, even in their favourite work of War, and their iron machinery—which at first brings outer prosperity and success—must be shown to be less lasting and effective than the living and flexible organisations of democratic Peoples. They must be proved failures before the world, so that the glamour of superficial successes may be destroyed for ever. They have had their day and their place in evolution, and have done their educative work. Now they are out-of-date, unfit for survival, and must vanish away.

The Case for India

When Great Britain sprang to arms, it was in defence of the freedom of a small nation, guaranteed by treaties, and the great principles she proclaimed electrified India and the Dominions. They all sprang to her side without question, without delay; they heard the voice of old England, the soldier of Liberty, and it thrilled their hearts. All were unprepared, save the small territorial army of Great Britain, due to the genius and foresight of Lord Haldane, and the readily mobilised army of India, hurled into the fray by the swift decision of Lord Hardinge. The little army of Britain fought for time; fought to stop the road to Paris, the heart of France; fought, falling back step by step, and gained the time it fought for, till India's sons stood on the soil of France, were flung to the front, rushed past the exhausted regiments who cheered them with failing breath, charged the advancing hosts, stopped the retreat, and joined the British army in forming that unbreakable line which wrestled to the death through two fearful winters—often, these soldiers of the tropics, waist-deep in freezing mud—and knew no surrender.

India, with her clear vision, saw in Great Britain the champion of Freedom, in Germany the champion of Despotism. And she saw rightly. Rightly she stood by Great Britain, despite her own lack of freedom and the coercive legislation which outrivalled German despotism, knowing these to be temporary, because un-English, and therefore doomed to destruction; she spurned the lure of German gold and rejected German appeals to revolt. She offered men and money; her educated classes, her Vakils, offered themselves as Volunteers, pleaded to be accepted. Then the never-sleeping distrust of Anglo-India rejected the offer, pressed for money, rejected men. And, slowly, educated India sank back, depressed and disheartened, and a splendid opportunity for knitting together the two Nations was lost.

Early in the War I ventured to say that the War could not end until England recognised that autocracy and bureaucracy must perish in India as well as in Europe. The good Bishop of Calcutta, with a courage worthy of his free race, lately declared that it would be hypocritical to pray for victory over autocracy in Europe and to maintain it in India. Now it has been clearly and definitely declared that Self-Government is to be the objective of Great Britain in India, and that a substantial measure of it is to be given at once; when this promise is made good by the granting of the Reforms outlined last year in Lucknow, then the end of the War will be in sight. For the War cannot end till the death-knell of autocracy is sounded.

Causes, with which I will deal presently and for which India was not responsible, have somewhat obscured the first eager expressions of India's sympathy, and have forced her thoughts largely towards her own position in the Empire. But that does not detract from the immense aid she has given, and is still giving. It must not be forgotten that long before the present War she had submitted—at first, while she had no power of remonstrance, and later, after 1885, despite the constant protests of Congress—to an ever-rising military expenditure, due partly to the amalgamation scheme of 1859, and partly to the cost of various wars beyond her frontiers, and to continual recurring frontier and trans-frontier expeditions, in which she had no real interest. They were sent out for supposed Imperial advantages, not for her own.

Between 1859 and 1904—45 years—Indian troops were engaged in thirty-seven wars and expeditions. There were ten wars: the two Chinese Wars of 1860 and 1900, the Bhutan War of 1864-65, the Abyssinian War of 1868, the Afghan War of 1878-79, and, after the massacre of the Kabul Mission, the second War of 1879-80, ending in an advance of the frontier, in the search for an ever receding "scientific frontier"; on this occasion the frontier was shifted, says Keene, "from the line of the Indus to the western slope of the Suleiman range and from Peshawar to Quetta"; the Egyptian War of 1882, in which the Indian troops markedly distinguished themselves; the third Burmese War of 1885 ending in the annexation of Upper Burma in 1886; the invasions of Tibet in 1890 and 1904. Of Expeditions, or minor Wars, there were 27; to Sitana in 1858 on a small scale and in 1863 on a larger (the "Sitana Campaign"); to Nepal and Sikkim in 1859; to Sikkim in 1864; a serious struggle on the North-west Frontier in 1868; expeditions against the Lushais in 1871-72, the Daflas in 1874-75, the Nagas in 1875, the Afridis in 1877, the Rampa Hill tribes in 1879, the Waziris and Nagas in 1881, the Akhas in 1884, and in the same year an expedition to the Zhob Valley, and a second thither in 1890. In 1888 and 1889 there was another expedition against Sikkim, against the Akozais (the Black Mountain Expedition) and against the Hill Tribes of the North-east, and in 1890 another Black Mountain Expedition, with a third in 1892. In 1890 came the expedition to Manipur, and in 1891 there was another expedition against the Lushais, and one into the Miranzal Valley. The Chitral Expedition occupied 1894-95, and the serious Tirah Campaign, in which 40,000 men were engaged, came in 1897 and 1898. The long list—which I have closed with 1904—ends with the expeditions against the Mahsuds in 1901, against the Kabalis in 1902, and the invasion of Tibet, before noted. All these events explain the rise in military expenditure, and we must add to them the sending of Indian troops to Malta and Cyprus in 1878—a somewhat theatrical demonstration—and the expenditure of some £2,000,000 to face what was described as "the Russian Menace" in 1884. Most of these were due to Imperial, not to Indian, policy, and many of the burdens imposed were protested against by the Government of India, while others were encouraged by ambitious Viceroys. I do not think that even this long list is complete.

Ever since the Government of India was taken over by the Crown, India has been regarded as an Imperial military asset and training ground, a position from which the jealousy of the East India Company had largely protected her, by insisting that the army it supported should be used for the defence and in the interests of India alone. Her value to the Empire for military purposes would not so seriously have injured at once her pride and her finances if the natural tendencies of her martial races had been permitted their previous scope; but the disarming of the people, 20 years after the assumption of the Government by the Crown, emasculated the Nation, and the elimination of races supposed to be unwarlike, or in some cases too warlike to be trusted, threw recruitment more and more to the north, and lowered the physique of the Bengalis and Madrasis, on whom the Company had largely depended.

The superiority of the Punjab, on which Sir Michael O'Dwyer so vehemently insisted the other day, is an artificial superiority, created by the British system and policy; and the poor recruitment elsewhere, on which he laid offensive insistence, is due to the same system and policy, which largely eliminated Bengalis, Madrasis and Mahrattas from the army. In Bengal, however, the martial type has been revived, chiefly in consequence of what the Bengalis felt to be the intolerable insult of the high-handed Partition of Bengal by Lord Curzon.

On this Gopal Krishna Gokhale said:

Bengal's heroic stand against the oppression of a harsh and uncontrolled bureaucracy has astonished and gratified all India.... All India owes a deep debt of gratitude to Bengal.

The spirit evoked showed itself in the youth of Bengal by a practical revolt, led by the elders, while it was confined to Swadeshi and Boycott, and rushing on, when it broke away from their authority, into conspiracy, assassination and dacoity: as had happened in similar revolts with Young Italy, in the days of Mazzini, and with Young Russia in the days of Stepniak and Kropotkin. The results of their despair, necessarily met by the halter and penal servitude, had to be faced by Lord Hardinge and Lord Carmichael during the present War. Other results, happy instead of disastrous in their nature, was the development of grit and endurance of a high character, shown in the courage of the Bengal lads in the serious floods that have laid parts of the Province deep under water, and in their compassion and self-sacrifice in the relief of famine. Their services in the present War—the Ambulance Corps and the replacement of its *materiel* when the ship carrying it sank, with the splendid services rendered by it in Mesopotamia; the recruiting of a Bengali regiment for active service, 900 strong, with another 900 reserves to replace wastage, and recruiting still going on—these are instances of the divine alchemy which brings the soul of good out of evil action, and consecrates to service the qualities evoked by rebellion.

In England, also, a similar result has been seen in a convict, released to go to the front, winning the Victoria Cross. It would be an act of statesmanship, as well as of divinest compassion, to offer to every prisoner and interned captive, held for political crime or on political suspicion, the opportunity of serving the Empire at the front. They might, if thought necessary, form a separate battalion or a separate regiment, under stricter supervision, and yet be given a chance of redeeming their reputation, for they are mostly very young.

The financial burden incurred in consequence of the above conflicts, and of other causes, now to be mentioned, would not have been so

The Case for India

much resented, if it had been imposed by India on herself, and if her own sons had profited by her being used as a training ground for the Empire. But in this case, as in so many others, she has shared Imperial burdens, while not sharing Imperial freedom and power. Apart from this, the change which made the Army so ruinous a burden on the resources of the country was the system of "British reliefs," the using of India as a training ground for British regiments, and the transfer of the men thus trained, to be replaced by new ones under the short service system, the cost of the frequent transfers and their connected expenses being charged on the Indian revenues, while the whole advantage was reaped by Great Britain. On the short service system the Simla Army Commission declared:

The short service system recently introduced into the British Army has increased the cost and has materially reduced the efficiency of the British troops in India. We cannot resist the feeling that, in the introduction of this system, the interest of the Indian tax-payer was entirely left out of consideration.

The remark was certainly justified, for the short service system gave India only five years of the recruits she paid heavily for and trained, all the rest of the benefit going to England. The latter was enabled, as the years went on, to enormously increase her Reserves, so that she has had 400,000 men trained in, and at the cost of, India.

In 1863 the Indian army consisted of 140,000 men, with 65,000 white officers. Great changes were made in 1885-1905, including the reorganisation under Lord Kitchener, who became Commander-in-Chief at the end of 1902. Even in this hasty review, I must not omit reference to the fact that Army Stores were drawn from Britain at enormous cost, while they should have been chiefly manufactured here, so that India might have profited by the expenditure. Lately under the necessities of War, factories have been turned to the production of munitions; but this should have been done long ago, so that India might have been enriched instead of exploited. The War has forced an investigation into her mineral resources that might have been made for her own sake, but Germany was allowed to monopolise the supply of minerals that India could have produced and worked up, and would have produced and worked up had she enjoyed Home Rule. India would have been richer, and the Empire safer, had she been a partner instead of a possession. But this side of the question will come under the matters directly affecting merchants, and we may venture to express a hope that the Government help extended to munition factories in time of War may be continued to industrial factories in time of Peace. The net result of the various causes above-mentioned was that the expense of the Indian army rose by leaps and bounds, until, before the War, India was expending £21,000,000 as against the £28,000,000 expended by the United Kingdom, while the wealthy Dominions of Canada and Australia were spending only 1-1/2 and 1-1/4 millions respectively. (I am not forgetting that the United Kingdom was expending over £51,000,000 on her Navy, while India was free of that burden, save for a contribution of half a million.)

Since 1885, the Congress has constantly protested against the ever-increasing military expenditure, but the voice of the Congress was supposed to be the voice of sedition and of class ambition, instead of being, as it was the voice of educated Indians, the most truly patriotic and loyal class of the population. In 1885, in the First Congress, Mr. P. Rangiah Naidu pointed out that military expenditure had been £1,463,000 in 1857 and had risen to £16,975,750 in 1884. Mr. D.E. Wacha ascribed the growth to the amalgamation scheme of 1859, and remarked that the Company in 1856 had an army of 254,000 men at a cost of 11-1/2 millions, while in 1884 the Crown had an army of only 181,000 men at a cost of 17 millions. The rise was largely due to the increased cost of the European regiments, overland transport service, stores, pensions, furlough allowances, and the like, most of them imposed despite the resistance of the Government of India, which complained that the changes were "made entirely, it may be said, from Imperial considerations, in which Indian interests have not been consulted or advanced." India paid nearly £700,000 a year, for instance, for "Home Depôts" — Home being England of course — in which lived some 20,000 to 22,000 British soldiers, on the plea that their regiments, not they, were serving in India. I cannot follow out the many increases cited by Mr. Wacha, but members can refer to his excellent speech.

Mr. Fawcett once remarked that when the East India Company was abolished the English people became directly responsible for the Government of India. It cannot, I think, be denied that this responsibility has been so imperfectly discharged that in many respects the new system of Government compares unfavourably with the old.... There was at that time an independent control of expenditure which now seems to be almost entirely wanting.

Shortly after the Crown assumed the rule of India, Mr. Disraeli asked the House of Commons to regard India as "a great and solemn trust committed to it by an all-wise and inscrutable Providence." Mr. George Yule, in the Fourth Congress, remarked on this: "The 650 odd members had thrown the trust back upon the hands of Providence, to be looked after as Providence itself thinks best." Perhaps it is time that India should remember that Providence helps those who help themselves.

Year after year the Congress continued to remonstrate against the cost of the army, until in 1902, after all the futile protests of the intervening years, it condemned an increase of pay to British soldiers in India which placed an additional burden on the Indian revenues of £786,000 a year, and pointed out that the British garrison was unnecessarily numerous, as was shown by the withdrawal of large bodies of British soldiers for service in South Africa and China. The very next year Congress protested that the increasing military expenditure was not to secure India against internal disorder or external attack, but in order to carry out an Imperial policy; the Colonies contributed little or nothing to the Imperial Military Expenditure, while India bore the cost of about one-third of the whole British Army in addition to her own Indian troops. Surely these facts should be remembered when India's military services to the Empire are now being weighed.

In 1904 and 1905, the Congress declared that the then military expenditure was beyond India's power to bear, and in the latter year prayed that the additional ten millions sterling sanctioned for Lord Kitchener's reorganisation scheme might be devoted to education and the reduction of the burden on the raiyats. In 1908, the burdens imposed by the British War Office since 1859 were condemned, and in the next year it was pointed out that the military expenditure was nearly a third of the whole Indian revenue, and was starving Education and Sanitation.

Lord Kitchener's reorganisation scheme kept the Indian Army on a War footing, ready for immediate mobilisation, and on January 1, 1915, the regular army consisted of 247,000 men, of whom 75,000 were English; it was the money spent by India in maintaining this army for years in readiness for War which made it possible for her to go to the help of Great Britain at the critical early period to which I alluded. She spent over £20 millions on the military services in 1914-15. In 1915-16 she spent £21.8 millions. In 1916-17 her military budget had risen to £12 millions, and it will probably be exceeded, as was the budget of the preceding year by £1-2/3 million.

Lord Hardinge, the last Viceroy of India, who is ever held in loving memory here for his sympathetic attitude towards Indian aspirations, made a masterly exposition of India's War services in the House of Lords on the third of last July. He emphasised her pre-War services, showing that though 19-1/4 millions sterling was fixed as a maximum by the Nicholson Committee, that amount had been exceeded in 11 out of the last 13 budgets, while his own last budget had risen to 22 millions. During these 13 years the revenue had been only between 48 and 58 millions, once rising to 60 millions. Could any fact speak more eloquently of India's War services than this proportion of military expenditure compared with her revenue?

The Great War began on August 4th, and in that very month and in the early part of September, India sent an expeditionary force of three divisions—two infantry and one cavalry—and another cavalry division joined them in France in November. The first arrived, said Lord Hardinge, "in time to fill a gap that could not otherwise have been filled." He added pathetically: "There are very few survivors of those two splendid divisions of infantry." Truly, their homes are empty, but their sons shall enjoy in India the liberty for which their fathers died in France. Three more divisions were at once sent to guard the Indian frontier, while in September a mixed division was sent to East Africa, and in October and November two more divisions and a brigade of cavalry went to Egypt. A battalion of Indian infantry went to Mauritius, another to the Cameroons, and two to the Persian Gulf, while other Indian troops helped the Japanese in the capture of Tsingtau. 210,000 Indians were thus sent overseas. The whole of these troops were fully armed and equipped, and in addition, during the first few weeks of the War, India sent to England from her magazines "70 million rounds of small-arm ammunition, 60,000 rifles, and more than 550 guns of the latest pattern and type."

In addition to these, Lord Hardinge speaks of sending to England

enormous quantities of material, ... tents, boots, saddlery, clothing, etc., but every effort was made to meet the ever-increasing demands made by the War Office, and it may be stated without exaggeration that India was bled absolutely white during the first few weeks of the war.

It must not be forgotten, though Lord Hardinge has not reckoned it, that all wastage has been more than filled up, and 450,000 men represent this head; the increase in units has been 300,000, and including other military items India had placed in the field up to the end of 1916 over a million of men.

In addition to this a British force of 80,000 was sent from India, fully trained and equipped at Indian cost, India receiving in exchange, many months later, 34 Territorial battalions and 29 batteries, "unfit for immediate employment on the frontier or in Mesopotamia, until they had been entirely re-armed and equipped, and their training completed."

Between the autumn of 1914 and the close of 1915, the defence of our own frontiers was a serious matter, and Lord Hardinge says:

The attitude of Afghanistan was for a long time doubtful, although I always had confidence in the personal loyalty of our ally the Amir; but I feared lest he might be overwhelmed by a wave of fanaticism, or by a successful Jehad of the tribes.... It suffices to mention that, although during the previous three years there had been no operations of any importance on the North-West frontier, there were, between November 29, 1914, and September 5, 1915, no less than seven serious attacks on the North-West frontier, all of which were effectively dealt with.

The military authorities had also to meet a German conspiracy early in 1915, 7,000 men arriving from Canada and the United States, having planned to seize points of military vantage in the Panjab, and in December of the same year another German conspiracy in Bengal, necessitating military preparations on land, and also naval patrols in the Bay of Bengal.

Lord Hardinge has been much attacked by the Tory and Unionist Press in England and India, in England because of the Mesopotamia Report, in India because his love for India brought him hatred from Anglo-India. India has affirmed her confidence in him, and with India's verdict he may well rest satisfied.

I do not care to dwell on the Mesopotamia Commission and its condemnation of the bureaucratic system prevailing here. Lord Hardinge vindicated himself and India. The bureaucratic system remains undefended. I recall that bureaucratic inefficiency came out in even more startling fashion in connection with the Afghan War of 1878-79 and 1879-80. In February 1880, the war charges were reported as under £4 millions, and the accounts showed a surplus of £2 millions. On April 8th the Government of India reported: "Outgoing for War very alarming, far exceeding estimate," and on the 13th April "it was announced that the cash balances had fallen in three months from thirteen crores to less than nine, owing to 'excessive Military drain' ... On the following day (April 22) a despatch was sent out to the Viceroy, showing that there appeared a deficiency of not less than 5-1/4 crores. This vast error was evidently due to an underestimate of war liabilities, which had led to such mis-information being laid before Parliament, and to the sudden discovery of inability to 'meet the usual drawings.'"

It seemed that the Government knew only the amount audited, not the amount spent. Payments were entered as "advances," though they were not recoverable, and "the great negligence was evidently that of the heads of departmental accounts." If such a mishap should occur under Home Rule, a few years hence — which heaven forbid — I shudder to think of the comments of the *Englishman* and the *Madras Mail* on the shocking inefficiency of Indian officials.

In September last, our present Viceroy, H.E. Lord Chelmsford, defended India against later attacks by critics who try to minimise her sacrifices in order to lessen the gratitude felt by Great Britain towards her, lest that gratitude should give birth to justice, and justice should award freedom to India. Lord Chelmsford placed before his Council "in studiously considered outline, a summary of what India has done during the past two years." Omitting his references to what was done under Lord Hardinge, as stated above, I may quote from him:

On the outbreak of war, of the 4,598 British officers on the Indian establishment, 530 who were at home on leave were detained by the War Office for service in Europe. 2,600 Combatant Officers have been withdrawn from India since the beginning of the War, excluding those who proceeded on service with their batteries or regiments. In order to make good these deficiencies and provide for war wastage the Indian Army Reserve of Officers was expanded from a total of 40, at which it stood on the 4th August, 1914, to one of 2,000.

The establishment of Indian units has not only been kept up to strength, but has been considerably increased. There has been an augmentation of 20 per cent. in the cavalry and of 40 per cent. in the infantry, while the number of recruits enlisted since the beginning of the War is greater than the entire strength of the Indian Army as it existed on August 4, 1914.

Lord Chelmsford rightly pointed out:

The Army in India has thus proved a great Imperial asset, and in weighing the value of India's contribution to the War it should be remembered that India's forces were no hasty improvisation, but were an army in being, fully equipped and supplied, which had previously cost India annually a large sum to maintain.

Lord Chelmsford has established what he calls a "Man-Power Board," the duty of which is "to collect and co-ordinate all the facts with regard to the supply of man-power in India." It has branches in all the Provinces. A steady flow of reinforcements supplies the wastage at the various fronts, and the labour required for engineering, transport, etc., is now organised in 20 corps in Mesopotamia and 25 corps in France. In addition 60,000 artisans, labourers, and specialists are serving in Mesopotamia and East Africa, and some 20,000 menials and followers have also gone overseas. Indian medical practitioners have accepted temporary commissions in the Indian Medical Service to the number of 500. In view of this fact, due to Great Britain's bitter need of help, may we not hope that this Service will welcome Indians in time of peace as well as in time of war, and will no longer bar the way by demanding the taking of a degree in the United Kingdom? It is also worthy of notice that the I.M.S. officers in charge of district duties have been largely replaced by Indian medical men; this, again, should continue after the War. Another fact, that the Army Reserve of Officers his risen from 40 to 2,000, suggests that the throwing open of King's Commissions to qualified Indians should not be represented by a meagre nine. If English lads of 19 and 20 are worthy of King's Commissions—and the long roll of slain Second Lieutenants proves it—then certainly Indian lads, since Indians have fought as bravely as Englishmen, should find the door thrown open to them equally widely in their own country, and the Indian Army should be led by Indian officers.

With such a record of deeds as the one I have baldly sketched, it is not necessary to say much in words as to India's support of Great Britain and her Allies. She has proved up to the hilt her desire to remain within the Empire, to maintain her tie with Great Britain. But if Britain is to call successfully on India's man-power, as Lord Chelmsford suggests in his Man-Power Board, then must the man who fights or labours have a man's Rights in his own land. The lesson which springs out of this War is that it is absolutely necessary for the future safety of the Empire that India shall have Home Rule. Had her Man-Power been utilised earlier there would have been no War, for none would have dared to provoke Great Britain and India to a contest. But her Man-Power cannot be utilised while she is a subject Nation. She cannot afford to maintain a large army, if she is to support an English garrison, to pay for their goings and comings, to buy stores in England at exorbitant prices and send them back again when England needs them. She cannot afford to train men for England, and only have their services for five years. She cannot afford to keep huge Gold Reserves in England, and be straitened for cash, while she lends to England out of her Reserves, taken from her over-taxation, £27,000,000 for War expenses, and this, be it remembered, before the great War Loan. I once said in England: "The condition of India's loyalty is India's freedom." I may now add: "The condition of India's usefulness to the Empire is India's freedom." She will tax herself willingly when her taxes remain in the country and fertilise it, when they educate her people and thus increase their productive power, when they foster her trade and create for her new industries.

The Case for India

Great Britain needs India as much as India needs England, for prosperity in Peace as well as for safety in War. Mr. Montagu has wisely said that "for equipment in War a Nation needs freedom in Peace." Therefore I say that, for both countries alike, the lesson of the War is Home Rule for India.

Let me close this part of my subject by laying at the feet of His Imperial Majesty the loving homage of the thousands here assembled, with the hope and belief that, ere long, we shall lay there the willing and grateful homage of a free Nation.

CHAPTER II.
CAUSES OF THE NEW SPIRIT IN INDIA.

Apart from the natural exchange of thought between East and West, the influence of English education, literature and ideals, the effect of travel in Europe, Japan and the United States of America, and other recognised causes for the changed outlook in India, there have been special forces at work during the last few years to arouse a New Spirit in India, and to alter her attitude of mind. These may be summed up as:

(*a*) The Awakening of Asia.

(*b*) Discussions abroad on Alien Rule and Imperial Reconstruction.

(*c*) Loss of Belief in the Superiority of the White Races.

(*d*) The Awakening of Indian Merchants.

(*e*) The Awakening of Indian Womanhood to claim its Ancient Position.

(*f*) The Awakening of the Masses.

Each of these causes has had its share in the splendid change of attitude in the Indian Nation, in the uprising of a spirit of pride of country, of independence, of self-reliance, of dignity, of self-respect. The War has quickened the rate of evolution of the world, and no country has experienced the quickening more than our Motherland.

THE AWAKENING OF ASIA.

In a conversation I had with Lord Minto, soon after his arrival as Viceroy, he discussed the so-called "unrest in India," and recognised it as the inevitable result of English Education, of English Ideals of Democracy, of the Japanese victory over Russia, and of the changing conditions in the outer world. I was therefore not surprised to read his remark that he recognised, "frankly and publicly, that new aspirations were stirring in the hearts of the people, that they were part of a larger movement common to the whole East, and that it was necessary to satisfy them to a reasonable extent by giving them a larger share in the administration."

But the present movement in India will be very poorly understood if it be regarded only in connexion with the movement in the East. The awakening of Asia is part of a world-movement, which has been quickened into marvellous rapidity by the world-war. The world-movement is towards Democracy, and for the West dates from the breaking away of the American Colonies from Great Britain, consummated in 1776, and its sequel in the French Revolution of 1789. Needless to say that its root was in the growth of modern science, undermining the fabric of intellectual servitude, in the work of the Encyclopædists, and in that of Jean-Jacques Rousseau and of Thomas Paine. In the East, the swift changes in Japan, the success of the Japanese Empire against Russia, the downfall of the Manchu dynasty in China and the establishment of a Chinese Republic, the efforts at improvement in Persia, hindered by the interference of Russia and Great Britain with their growing ambitions, and the creation of British and Russian "spheres of influence," depriving her of her just liberty, and now the Russian Revolution and the probable rise of a Russian Republic in Europe and Asia, have all entirely changed the conditions before existing in India. Across Asia, beyond the Himalayas, stretch free and self-ruling Nations. India no longer sees as her Asian neighbours the huge domains of a Tsar and a Chinese despot, and compares her condition under British rule with those of their subject populations. British rule profited by the comparison, at least until 1905, when the great period of repression set in. But in future, unless India wins Self-Government, she will look enviously at her Self-Governing neighbours, and the contrast will intensify her unrest.

But even if she gains Home Rule, as I believe she will, her position in the Empire will imperatively demand that she shall be strong as well as free. She becomes not only a vulnerable point in the Empire, as the Asian Nations evolve their own ambitions and rivalries, but also a possession to be battled for. Mr. Laing once said: "India is the milch-cow of England," a Kamadhenu, in fact, a cow of plenty; and if that view should arise in Asia, the ownership of the milch-cow would become a matter of dispute, as of old between Vashishtha and Vishvamitra. Hence India must be capable of self-defence both by land and sea. There may be a struggle for the primacy of Asia, for supremacy in the Pacific, for the mastery of Australasia, to say nothing of the inevitable trade-struggles, in which Japan is already endangering Indian industry and Indian trade, while India is unable to protect herself.

In order to face these larger issues with equanimity, the Empire requires a contented, strong, self-dependent and armed India, able to hold her own and to aid the Dominions, especially Australia, with her small population and immense unoccupied and undefended area. India alone has the man-power which can effectively maintain the Empire in Asia, and it is a short-sighted, a criminally short-sighted, policy not to build up her strength as a Self-Governing State within the Commonwealth of Free Nations under the British Crown. The Englishmen in India talk loudly of their interests; what can this mere handful do to protect their interests against attack in the coming years? Only in a free and powerful India will they be safe. Those who read Japanese papers know how strongly, even during the War, they parade unchecked their pro-German sympathies, and how likely after the War is an alliance between these two ambitious and warlike Nations. Japan will come out of the War with her army and navy unweakened, and her trade immensely strengthened. Every consideration of sane statesmanship should lead Great Britain to trust India more than Japan, so that the British Empire in Asia may rest on the sure foundation of Indian loyalty, the loyalty of a free and contented people, rather than be dependent on the continued friendship of a possible future rival. For international friendships are governed by National interests, and are built on quicksands, not on rock.

Englishmen in India must give up the idea that English dominance is necessary for the protection of their interests, amounting, in 1915, to £365,399,000 sterling. They do not claim to dominate the United States of America, because they have invested there £688,078,000. They do not claim to dominate the Argentine Republic, because they have invested there £269,808,000. Why then should they claim to dominate India on the ground of their investment? Britons must give up the idea that India is a possession to be exploited for their own benefit, and must see her as a friend, an equal, a Self-Governing Dominion within the Empire, a Nation like themselves, a willing partner in the Empire, and not a dependent. The democratic movement in Japan, China and

Russia in Asia has sympathetically affected India, and it is idle to pretend that it will cease to affect her.

DISCUSSIONS ABROAD ON ALIEN RULE AND IMPERIAL RECONSTRUCTION.

But there are other causes which have been working in India, consequent on the British attitude against autocracy and in defence of freedom in Europe, while her attitude to India has, until lately, been left in doubt. Therefore I spoke of a splendid opportunity lost. India at first believed whole-heartedly that Great Britain was fighting for the freedom of all Nationalities. Even now, Mr. Asquith declared—in his speech in the House of Commons reported here last October, on the peace resolution of Mr. Ramsay Macdonald—that "the Allies are fighting for nothing but freedom, and, an important addition—for nothing short of freedom." In his speech declaring that Britain would stand by France in her claim for the restoration of Alsace-Lorraine, he spoke of "the intolerable degradation of a foreign yoke." Is such a yoke less intolerable, less wounding to self-respect here, than in Alsace-Lorraine, where the rulers and the ruled are both of European blood, similar in religion and habits? As the War went on, India slowly and unwillingly came to realise that the hatred of autocracy was confined to autocracy in the West, and that the degradation was only regarded as intolerable for men of white races; that freedom was lavishly promised to all except to India; that new powers were to be given to the Dominions, but not to India. India was markedly left out of the speeches of statesmen dealing with the future of the Empire, and at last there was plain talk of the White Empire, the Empire of the Five Nations, and the "coloured races" were lumped together as the wards of the White Empire, doomed to an indefinite minority.

The peril was pressing; the menace unmistakable. The Reconstruction of the Empire was on the anvil; what was to be India's place therein? The Dominions were proclaimed as partners; was India to remain a Dependency? Mr. Bonar Law bade the Dominions strike while the iron was hot; was India to wait till it was cold? India saw her soldiers fighting for freedom in Flanders, in France, in Gallipoli, in Asia Minor, in China, in Africa; was she to have no share of the freedom for which she fought? At last she sprang to her feet and cried, in the words of one of her noblest sons: "Freedom is my birthright; and I want it." The words "Home Rule" became her Mantram. She claimed her place in the Empire.

Thus, while she continued to support, and even to increase, her army abroad, fighting for the Empire, and poured out her treasures as water for Hospital Ships, War Funds, Red Cross organisations, and the gigantic War Loan, a dawning fear oppressed her, lest, if she did not take order with her own household, success in the War for the Empire might mean decreased liberty for herself.

The recognition of the right of the Indian Government to make its voice heard in Imperial matters, when they were under discussion in an Imperial Conference, was a step in the right direction. But disappointment was felt that while other countries were represented by responsible Ministers, the representation in India's case was of the Government, of a Government irresponsible to her, and not the representative of herself. No fault was found with the choice itself, but only with the non-representative character of the chosen, for they were selected by the Government, and not by the elected members of the Supreme Council. This defect in the resolution moved by the Hon. Khan Bahadur M.M. Shafi on October 2, 1915, was pointed out by the Hon. Mr. Surendranath Bannerji. He said:

My Lord, in view of a situation so full of hope and promise, it seems to me that my friend's Resolution does not go far enough. He pleads for *official* representation at the Imperial Conference: he does not plead for *popular* representation. He urges that an address be presented to His Majesty's Government, through the Secretary of State for India, for official representation at the Imperial Council. My Lord, official representation may mean little or nothing. It may indeed be attended with some risk; for I am sorry to have to say—but say it I must—that our officials do not always see eye to eye with us as regards many great public questions which affect this country; and indeed their views, judged from our standpoint, may sometimes seem adverse to our interests. At the same time, my Lord, I recognise the fact that the Imperial Conference is an assemblage of officials pure and simple, consisting of Ministers of the United Kingdom and of the self-governing Colonies. But, my Lord, there is an essential difference between them and ourselves. In their case, the Ministers are the elect of the people, their organ and their voice, answerable to them for their conduct and their proceedings. In our case, our officials are public servants in name, but in reality they are the masters of the public. The situation may improve, and I trust it will, under the liberalising influence of your Excellency's beneficent administration; but we must take things as they are, and not indulge in building castles in the air, which may vanish "like the baseless fabric of a vision."

It was said to be an epoch-making event that "Indian Representatives" took part in the Conference. Representatives they were, but, as said, of the British Government in India, not of India, whereas their colleagues represented their Nations. They did good work, none the less, for they were able and experienced men, though they failed us in the Imperial Preference Conference and, partially, on the Indentured Labour question. Yet we hope that the presence in the Conference of men of Indian birth may prove to be the proverbial "thin end of the wedge," and may have convinced their colleagues that, while India was still a Dependency, India's sons were fully their equals.

The Report of the Public Services Commission, though now too obviously obsolete to be discussed, caused both disappointment and resentment; for it showed that, in the eyes of the majority of the Commissioners, English domination in Indian administration was to be perpetual, and that thirty years hence she would only hold a pitiful 25 per cent. of the higher appointments in the I.C.S. and the Police. I cannot, however, mention that Commission, even in passing, without voicing India's thanks to the Hon. Mr. Justice Rahim, for his rare courage in writing a solitary Minute of Dissent, in which he totally rejected the Report, and laid down the right principles which should govern recruitment for the Indian Civil Services.

India had but three representatives on the Commission; G.K. Gokhale died ere it made its Report, his end quickened by his sufferings during its work, by the humiliation of the way in which his countrymen were treated. Of Mr. Abdur Rahim I have already spoken. The Hon. Mr. M.B. Chaubal signed the Report, but dissented from some of its most important recommendations. The whole Report was written "before the flood," and it is now merely an antiquarian curiosity.

India, for all these reasons, was forced to see before her a future of perpetual subordination: the Briton rules in Great Britain, the Frenchman in France, the American in America, each Dominion in its own area, but the Indian was to rule nowhere; alone among the peoples of the world, he was not to feel his own country as his own. "Britain for the British" was right and natural; "India for the Indians" was wrong, even seditious. It must be "India for the Empire," or not even for the Empire, but "for the rest of the Empire," careless of herself. "British support for British Trade" was patriotic and proper in Britain. "Swadeshi goods for Indians" showed a petty and anti-Imperial spirit in India. The Indian was to continue to live perpetually, and even thankfully, as Gopal Krishna Gokhale said he lived now, in "an atmosphere of inferiority," and to be proud to be a citizen (without rights) of the Empire, while its other component Nations were to be citizens (with rights) in their own countries first, and citizens of the Empire secondarily. Just as his trust in Great Britain was strained nearly to breaking point came the glad news of Mr. Montagu's appointment as Secretary of State for India, of the Viceroy's invitation to him, and of his coming to hear for himself what India wanted. It was a ray of sunshine breaking through the gloom, confidence in Great Britain revived, and glad preparation was made to welcome the coming of a friend.

The attitude of India has changed to meet the changed attitude of the Governments of India and Great Britain. But let none imagine that that consequential change of attitude connotes any change in her determination to win Home Rule. She is ready to consider terms of peace, but it must be "peace with honour," and honour in this connection means Freedom. If this be not granted, an even more vigorous agitation will begin.

LOSS OF BELIEF IN THE SUPERIORITY OF WHITE RACES

The undermining of this belief dates from the spreading of the Arya Samaj and the Theosophical Society. Both bodies sought to lead the Indian people to a sense of the value of their own civilisation, to pride in their past, creating self-respect in the present, and self-confidence in the future. They destroyed the unhealthy inclination to imitate the West in all things, and taught discrimination, the using only of what was valuable in western thought and culture, instead of a mere slavish copying of everything. Another great force was that of Swami Vivekananda, alike in his passionate love and admiration for India,

The Case for India

and his exposure of the evils resulting from Materialism in the West. Take the following:

Children of India, I am here to speak to you to-day about some practical things, and my object in reminding you about the glories of the past is simply this. Many times have I been told that looking into the past only degenerates and leads to nothing, and that we should look to the future. That is true. But out of the past is built the future. Look back, therefore, as far as you can, drink deep of the eternal fountains that are behind, and after that, look forward, march forward, and make India brighter, greater, much higher than she ever was. Our ancestors were great. We must recall that. We must learn the elements of our being, the blood that courses in our veins; we must have faith in that blood, and what it did in the past: and out of that faith, and consciousness of past greatness, we must build an India yet greater than what she has been.

And again:

I know for certain that millions, I say deliberately, millions, in every civilised land are waiting for the message that will save them from the hideous abyss of materialism into which modern money-worship is driving them headlong, and many of the leaders of the new Social Movements have already discovered that Vedanta in its highest form can alone spiritualise their social aspirations.

The process was continued by the admiration of Sanskrit literature expressed by European scholars and philosophers. But the effect of these was confined to the few and did not reach the many. The first great shock to the belief in white superiority came from the triumph of Japan over Russia, the facing of a huge European Power by a comparatively small Eastern Nation, the exposure of the weakness and rottenness of the Russian leaders, and the contrast with their hardy virile opponents, ready to sacrifice everything for their country.

The second great shock has come from the frank brutality of German theories of the State, and their practical carrying out in the treatment of conquered districts and the laying waste of evacuated areas in retreat. The teachings of Bismarck and their practical application in France, Flanders, Belgium, Poland, and Serbia have destroyed all the glamour of the superiority of Christendom over Asia. Its vaunted civilisation is seen to be but a thin veneer, and its religion a matter of form rather than of life. Gazing from afar at the ghastly heaps of dead and the hosts of the mutilated, at science turned into devilry and ever inventing new tortures for rending and slaying, Asia may be forgiven for thinking that, on the whole, she prefers her own religions and her own civilisations.

But even deeper than the outer tumult of war has pierced the doubt as to the reality of the Ideals of Liberty and Nationality so loudly proclaimed by the foremost western Nations, the doubt of the honesty of their champions. Sir James Meston said truly, a short time ago, that he had never, in his long experience, known Indians in so distrustful and suspicious a mood as that which he met in them to-day. And that is so. For long years Indians have been chafing over the many breaches of promises and pledges to them that remain unredeemed. The maintenance here of a system of political repression, of coercive measures increased in number and more harshly applied since 1905, the carrying of the system to a wider extent since the War for the sanctity of treaties and for the protection of Nationalities has been going on, have deepened the mistrust. A frank and courageous statesmanship applied to the honest carrying out of large reforms too long delayed can alone remove it. The time for political tinkering is past; the time for wise and definite changes is here.

To these deep causes must be added the comparison between the progressive policy of some of the Indian States in matters which most affect the happiness of the people, and the slow advance made under British administration. The Indian notes that this advance is made under the guidance of rulers and ministers of his own race. When he sees that the suggestions made in the People's Assembly in Mysore are fully considered and, when possible, given effect to, he realises that without the forms of power the members exercise more real power than those in our Legislative Councils. He sees education spreading, new industries fostered, villagers encouraged to manage their own affairs and take the burden of their own responsibility, and he wonders why Indian incapacity is so much more efficient than British capacity.

Perhaps, after all, for Indians, Indian rule may be the best.

The Case for India

THE AWAKENING OF THE MERCHANTS.

THE AWAKENING OF INDIAN WOMANHOOD.

The position of women in the ancient Aryan civilisation was a very noble one. The great majority married, becoming, as Manu said, the Light of the Home; some took up the ascetic life, remained unmarried, and sought the knowledge of Brahma. The story of the Rani Damayanti, to whom her husband's ministers came, when they were troubled by the Raja's gambling, that of Gandhari, in the Council of Kings and Warrior Chiefs, remonstrating with her headstrong son; in later days, of Padmavati of Chitoor, of Mirabai of Marwar, the sweet poetess, of Tarabai of Thoda, the warrior, of Chand Bibi, the defender of Ahmednagar, of Ahalya Bai of Indore, the great Ruler—all these and countless others are well known.

Only in the last two or three generations have Indian women slipped away from their place at their husbands' side, and left them unhelped in their public life. But even now they wield great influence over husband and son. Culture has never forsaken them, but the English education of their husbands and sons, with the neglect of Sanskrit and the Vernacular, have made a barrier between the culture of the husband and that of the wife, and has shut the woman out from her old sympathy with the larger life of men. While the interests of the husband have widened, those of the wife have narrowed. The materialising of the husband tended also, by reaction, to render the wife's religion less broad and wise.

The wish to save their sons from the materialising results of English education awoke keen sympathy among Indian mothers with the movement to make religion an integral part of education. It was, perhaps, the first movement in modern days which aroused among them in all parts a keen and living interest.

The Partition of Bengal was bitterly resented by Bengali women, and was another factor in the outward-turning change. When the editor of an Extremist newspaper was prosecuted for sedition, convicted and sentenced, five hundred Bengali women went to his mother to show their sympathy, not by condolences, but by congratulations. Such was the feeling of the well-born women of Bengal.

Then the troubles of Indians outside India roused the ever quick sympathy of Indian women, and the attack in South Africa on the sacredness of Indian marriage drew large numbers of them out of their homes to protest against the wrong.

The Indentured Labour question, involving the dishonour of women, again, moved them deeply, and even sent a deputation to the Viceroy composed of women.

These were, perhaps, the chief outer causes; but deep in the heart of India's daughters arose the Mother's voice, calling on them to help Her to arise, and to be once more mistress in Her own household. Indian women, nursed on Her old literature, with its wonderful ideals of womanly perfection, could not remain indifferent to the great movement for India's liberty. And during the last few years the hidden fire, long burning in their hearts, fire of love to Bharatamata, fire of resentment against the lessened influence of the religion which they passionately love, instinctive dislike of the foreigner as ruling in their land, have caused a marvellous awakening. The strength of the Home Rule movement is rendered tenfold greater by the adhesion to it of large numbers of women, who bring to its helping the uncalculating heroism, the endurance, the self-sacrifice, of the feminine nature. Our League's best recruits are among the women of India, and the women of Madras boast that they marched in procession when the men were stopped, and that their prayers in the temples set the interned captives free. Home Rule has become so intertwined with religion by the prayers offered up in the great Southern Temples, sacred places of pilgrimage, and spreading from them to village temples, and also by its being preached up and down the country by Sadhus and Sannyasins, that it has become in the minds of the women and of the ever religious masses, inextricably intertwined with religion. That is, in this country, the surest way of winning alike the women of the higher classes and the men and women villagers. And that is why I have said that the two words, "Home Rule," have become a Mantram.

THE AWAKENING OF THE MASSES.

CHAPTER III.
WHY INDIA DEMANDS HOME RULE.

India demands Home Rule for two reasons, one essential and vital, the other less important but necessary: Firstly, because Freedom is the birthright of every Nation; secondly, because her most important interests are now made subservient to the interests of the British Empire without her consent, and her resources are not utilised for her greatest needs. It is enough only to mention the money spent on her Army, not for local defence but for Imperial purposes, as compared with that spent on primary education.

I. THE VITAL REASON.

What is a Nation?

Self-Government is necessary to the self-respect and dignity of a People; Other-Government emasculates a Nation, lowers its character, and lessens its capacity. The wrong done by the Arms Act, which Raja Rampal Singh voiced in the Second Congress as a wrong which outweighed all the benefits of British Rule, was its weakening and debasing effect on Indian manhood. "We cannot," he declared, "be grateful to it for degrading our natures, for systematically crushing out all martial spirit, for converting a race of soldiers and heroes into a timid flock of quill-driving sheep." This was done not by the fact that a man did not carry arms—few carry them in England—but that men were deprived of the *right* to carry them. A Nation, an individual, cannot develop his capacities to the utmost without liberty. And this is recognised everywhere except in India. As Mazzini truly said:

God has written a line of His thought over the cradle of every people. That is its special mission. It cannot be cancelled; it must be freely developed.

For what is a Nation? It is a spark of the Divine Fire, a fragment of the Divine Life, outbreathed into the world, and gathering round itself a mass of individuals, men, women and children, whom it binds together into one. Its qualities, its powers, in a word, its type, depend on the fragment of the Divine Life embodied in it, the Life which shapes it, evolves it, colours it, and makes it One. The magic of

The Case for India

Nationality is the feeling of oneness, and the use of Nationality is to serve the world in the particular way for which its type fits it. This is what Mazzini called "its special mission," the duty given to it by God in its birth-hour. Thus India had the duty of spreading the idea of Dharma, Persia that of Purity, Egypt that of Science, Greece that of Beauty, Rome that of Law. But to render its full service to Humanity it must develop along its own lines, and be Self-determined in its evolution. It must be Itself, and not Another. The whole world suffers where a Nationality is distorted or suppressed, before its mission to the world is accomplished.

The Cry for Self-Rule.

Hence the cry of a Nation for Freedom, for Self-Rule, is not a cry of mere selfishness demanding more Rights that it may enjoy more happiness. Even in that there is nothing wrong, for happiness means fulness of life, and to enjoy such fulness is a righteous claim. But the demand for Self-Rule is a demand for the evolution of its own nature for the Service of Humanity. It is a demand of the deepest Spirituality, an expression of the longing to give its very best to the world. Hence dangers cannot check it, nor threats appal, nor offerings of greater pleasures lure it to give up its demand for Freedom. In the adapted words of a Christian Scripture, it passionately cries: "What shall it profit a Nation if it gain the whole world and lose its own Soul? What shall a Nation give in exchange for its Soul?" Better hardship and freedom, than luxury and thraldom. This is the spirit of the Home Rule movement, and therefore it cannot be crushed, it cannot be destroyed, it is eternal and ever young. Nor can it be persuaded to exchange its birthright for any mess of efficiency-pottage at the hands of the bureaucracy.

Stunting the Race.

Coming closer to the daily life of the people as individuals, we see that the character of each man, woman and child is degraded and weakened by a foreign administration, and this is most keenly felt by the best Indians. Speaking on the employment of Indians in the Public Services, Gopal Krishna Gokhale said:

A kind of dwarfing or stunting of the Indian race is going on under the present system. We must live all the days of our life in an atmosphere of inferiority, and the tallest of us must bend, in order that the exigencies of the system may be satisfied. The upward impulse, if I may use such an expression, which every schoolboy at Eton or Harrow may feel that he may one day be a Gladstone, a Nelson, or a Wellington, and which may draw forth the best efforts of which he is capable, that is denied to us. The full height to which our manhood is capable of rising can never be reached by us under the present system. The moral elevation which every Self-governing people feel cannot be felt by us. Our administrative and military talents must gradually disappear owing to sheer disuse, till at last our lot, as hewers of wood and drawers of water in our own country, is stereotyped.

The Hon. Mr. Bhupendranath Basu has spoken on similar lines:

A bureaucratic administration, conducted by an imported agency, and centring all power in its hands, and undertaking all responsibility, has acted as a dead weight on the Soul of India, stifling in us all sense of initiative, for the lack of which we are condemned, atrophying the nerves of action and, what is more serious, necessarily dwarfing in us all feeling of self-respect.

In this connexion the warning of Lord Salisbury to Cooper's Hill students is significant:

No system of Government can be permanently safe where there is a feeling of inferiority or of mortification affecting the relations between the governing and the governed. There is nothing I would more earnestly wish to impress upon all who leave this country for the purpose of governing India than that, if they choose to be so, they are the only enemies England has to fear. They are the persons who can, if they will, deal a blow of the deadliest character at the future rule of England.

I have ventured to urge this danger, which has increased of late years, in consequence of the growing self-respect of the Indians, but the ostrich policy is thought to be preferable in my part of the country.

This stunting of the race begins with the education of the child. The Schools differentiate between British and Indian teachers; the Colleges do the same. The students see first-class Indians superseded by young and third-rate foreigners; the Principal of a College should be a foreigner; foreign history is more important than Indian; to have written on English villages is a qualification for teaching economics in India; the whole atmosphere of the School and College emphasises the superiority of the foreigner, even when the professors abstain from open assertion thereof. The Education Department controls the education given, and it is planned on foreign models, and its object is to serve foreign rather than native ends, to make docile Government servants rather than patriotic citizens; high spirits, courage, self-respect, are not encouraged, and docility is regarded as the most precious quality in the student; pride in country, patriotism, ambition, are looked on as dangerous, and English, instead of Indian, Ideals are exalted; the blessings of a foreign rule and the incapacity of Indians to manage their own affairs are constantly inculcated. What wonder that boys thus trained often turn out, as men, time-servers and sycophants, and, finding their legitimate ambitions frustrated, become selfish and care little for the public weal? Their own inferiority has been so driven into them during their most impressionable years, that they do not even feel what Mr. Asquith called the "intolerable degradation of a foreign yoke."

India's Rights.

It is not a question whether the rule is good or bad. German efficiency in Germany is far greater than English efficiency in England; the Germans were better fed, had more amusements and leisure, less crushing poverty than the English. But would any Englishman therefore desire to see Germans occupying all the highest positions in England? Why not? Because the righteous self-respect and dignity of the free man revolt against foreign domination, however superior. As Mr. Asquith said at the beginning of the War, such a condition was "inconceivable and would be intolerable." Why then is it the one conceivable system here in India? Why is it not felt by all Indians to be intolerable? It is because it has become a habit, bred in us from childhood, to regard the sahib-log as our natural superiors, and the greatest injury British rule has done to Indians is to deprive them of the natural instinct born in all free peoples, the feeling of an inherent right to Self-determination, to be themselves. Indian dress, Indian food, Indian ways, Indian customs, are all looked on as second-rate; Indian mother-tongue and Indian literature cannot make an educated man. Indians as well as Englishmen take it for granted that the natural rights of every Nation do not belong to them; they claim "a larger share in the government of the country," instead of claiming the government of their own country, and they are expected to feel grateful for "boons," for concessions. Britain is to say what she will give. The whole thing is wrong, topsy-turvy, irrational. Thank God that India's eyes are opening; that myriads of her people realise that they are men, with a man's right to freedom in his own country, a man's right to manage his own affairs. India is no longer on her knees for boons; she is on her feet for Rights. It is because I have taught this that the English in India misunderstand me and call me seditious; it is because I have taught this that I am President of this Congress to-day.

This may seem strong language, because the plain truth is not usually put in India. But this is what every Briton feels in Britain for his own country, and what every Indian should feel in India for his. This is the Freedom for which the Allies are fighting; this is Democracy, the Spirit of the Age. And this is what every true Briton will feel is India's Right the moment India claims it for herself, as she is claiming it now. When this right is gained, then will the tie between India and Great Britain become a golden link of mutual love and service, and the iron chain of a foreign yoke will fall away. We shall live and work side by side, with no sense of distrust and dislike, working as brothers for common ends. And from that union shall arise the mightiest Empire, or rather Commonwealth, that the world has ever known, a Commonwealth that, in God's good time, shall put an end to War.

II. THE SECONDARY REASONS.

Tests of Efficiency.

The Secondary Reasons for the present demand for Home Rule may be summed up in the blunt statement: "The present rule, while efficient in less important matters and in those which concern British interests, is inefficient in the greater matters on which the healthy life and happiness of the people depend." Looking at outer things, such as external order, posts and telegraphs—except where political agitators are concerned—main roads, railways, etc., foreign visitors, who expected to find a semi-savage country, hold up their hands in admiration. But if they saw the life of the people, the masses of struggling clerks trying to educate their children on Rs. 25 (28s. 0-1/4d.) a month, the masses of labourers with one meal a day, and the

The Case for India

huts in which they live, they would find cause for thought. And if the educated men talked freely with them, they would be surprised at their bitterness. Gopal Krishna Gokhale put the whole matter very plainly in 1911:

One of the fundamental conditions of the peculiar position of the British Government in this country is that it should be a continuously progressive Government. I think all thinking men, to whatever community they belong, will accept that. Now, I suggest four tests to judge whether the Government is progressive, and, further, whether it is continuously progressive. The first test that I would apply is what measures it adopts for the moral and material improvement of the mass of the people, and under these measures I do not include those appliances of modern Governments which the British Government has applied in this country, because they were appliances necessary for its very existence, though they have benefited the people, such as the construction of Railways, the introduction of Post and Telegraphs, and things of that kind. By measures for the moral and material improvement of the people, I mean what the Government does for education, what the Government does for sanitation, what the Government does for agricultural development, and so forth. That is my first test. The second test that I would apply is what steps the Government takes to give us a larger share in the administration of our local affairs—in municipalities and local boards. My third test is what voice the Government gives us in its Councils—in those deliberate assemblies, where policies are considered. And, lastly, we must consider how far Indians are admitted into the ranks of the public service.

A Change of System Needed.

Those were Gokhale's tests, and Indians can supply the results of their knowledge and experience to answer them. But before dealing with the failure to meet these tests, it is necessary to state here that it is not a question of blaming men, or of substituting Indians for Englishmen, but of changing the system itself. It is a commonplace that the best men become corrupted by the possession of irresponsible power. As Bernard Houghton says: "The possession of unchecked power corrupts some of the finer qualities." Officials quite honestly come to believe that those who try to change the system are undermining the security of the State. They identify the State with themselves, so that criticism of them is seen as treason to the State. The phenomenon is well known in history, and it is only repeating itself in India. The same writer—I prefer to use his words rather than my own, for he expresses exactly my own views, and will not be considered to be prejudiced as I am thought to be—cogently remarks:

He (the official) has become an expert in reports and returns and matters of routine through many years of practice. They are the very woof and warp of his brain. He has no ideas, only reflexes. He views with acrid disfavour untried conceptions. From being constantly preoccupied with the manipulation of the machine he regards its smooth working, the ordered and harmonious regulation of glittering pieces of machinery, as the highest service he can render to the country of his adoption. He determines that his particular cog-wheel at least shall be bright, smooth, silent, and with absolutely no backlash. Not unnaturally in course of time he comes to envisage the world through the strait embrasure of an office window. When perforce he must report on new proposals he will place in the forefront, not their influence on the life and progress of the people, but their convenience to the official hierarchy and the manner in which they affect its authority. Like the monks of old, or the squire in the typical English village, he cherishes a benevolent interest in the commonalty, and is quite willing, even eager, to take a general interest in their welfare, if only they do not display initiative or assert themselves in opposition to himself or his order. There is much in this proviso. Having come to regard his own judgment as almost divine, and the hierarchy of which he has the honour to form a part as a sacrosanct institution, he tolerates the laity so long as they labour quietly and peaceably at their vocations and do not presume to inter-meddle in high matters of State. That is the heinous offence. And frank criticism of official acts touches a lower depth still, even *lèse majesté*. For no official will endure criticism from his subordinates, and the public, who lie in outer darkness beyond the pale, do not in his estimation rank even with his subordinates. How, then, should he listen with patience when in their cavilling way they insinuate that, in spite of the labours of a high-souled bureaucracy, all is perhaps not for the best in the best of all possible worlds—still less when they suggest reforms that had never occurred even to him or to his order, and may clash with his most cherished ideals? It is for the officials to govern the country; they alone have been initiated into the sacred mysteries; they alone understand the secret working of the machine. At the utmost the laity may tender respectful and humble suggestions for their consideration, but no more. As for those who dare to think and act for themselves, their ignorant folly is only equalled by their arrogance. It is as though a handful of schoolboys were to dictate to their masters alterations in the traditional time-table, or to insist on a modified curriculum.... These worthy people [officials] confuse manly independence with disloyalty; they cannot conceive of natives except either as rebels or as timid sheep.

Non-Official Anglo-Indians.

The problem becomes more complicated by the existence in India of a small but powerful body of the same race as the higher officials; there are only 122,919 English-born persons in this country, while there are 245,000,000 in the British Raj and another 70,000,000 in the Indian States, more or less affected by British influence. As a rule, the non-officials do not take any part in politics, being otherwise occupied; but they enter the field when any hope arises in Indian hearts of changes really beneficial to the Nation. John Stuart Mill observed on this point:

The individuals of the ruling people who resort to the foreign country to make their fortunes are of all others those who most need to be held under powerful restraint. They are always one of the chief difficulties of the Government. Armed with the prestige and filled with the scornful overbearingness of the conquering Nation, they have the feelings inspired by absolute power without its sense of responsibility.

Similarly, Sir John Lawrence wrote:

The difficulty in the way of the Government of India acting fairly in these matters is immense. If anything is done, or attempted to be done, to help the natives, a general howl is raised, which reverberates in England, and finds sympathy and support there. I feel quite bewildered sometimes what to do. Everyone is, in the abstract, for justice, moderation, and suchlike excellent qualities; but when one comes to apply such principles so as to affect anybody's interests, then a change comes over them.

The Case for India

Keene, speaking of the principle of treating equally all classes of the community, says:

The application of that maxim, however, could not be made without sometimes provoking opposition among the handful of white settlers in India who, even when not connected with the administration, claimed a kind of class ascendancy which was not only in the conditions of the country but also in the nature of the case. It was perhaps natural that in a land of caste the compatriots of the rulers should become—as Lord Lytton said—a kind of "white Brahmanas"; and it was certain that, as a matter of fact, the pride of race and the possession of western civilisation created a sense of superiority, the display of which was ungraceful and even dangerous, when not tempered by official responsibility. This feeling had been sensitive enough in the days of Lord William Bentinck, when the class referred to was small in numbers and devoid of influence. It was now both more numerous, and—by reason of its connection with the newspapers of Calcutta and of London—it was far better able to make its passion heard.

During Lord Ripon's sympathetic administration the great outburst occurred against the Ilbert Bill in 1883. We are face to face with a similar phenomenon to-day, when we see the European Associations—under the leadership of the *Madras Mail*, the *Englishman* of Calcutta, the *Pioneer of* Allahabad, the *Civil and Military Gazette* of Lahore, with their Tory and Unionist allies in the London Press and with the aid of retired Indian officials and non-officials in England—desperately resisting the Reforms now proposed. Their opposition, we know, is a danger to the movement towards Freedom, and even when they have failed to impress England—as they are evidently failing—they will try to minimise or smother here the reforms which a statute has embodied. The Minto-Morley reforms were thus robbed of their usefulness, and a similar attempt, if not guarded against, will be made when the Congress-League Scheme is used as the basis for an Act.

The Re-action on England.

We cannot leave out of account here the deadly harm done to England herself by this un-English system of rule in India. Mr. Hobson has pointed out:

The Case for India

As our free Self-Governing Colonies have furnished hope, encouragement, and leading to the popular aspirations in Great Britain, not merely by practical success in the art of Self-Government, but by the wafting of a spirit of freedom and equality, so our despotically ruled Dependencies have ever served to damage the character of our people by feeding the habits of snobbish subservience, the admiration of wealth and rank, the corrupt survivals of the inequalities of feudalism.... Cobden writing in 1860 of our Indian Empire, put this pithy question: "Is it not just possible that we may become corrupted at home by the reaction of arbitrary political maxims in the East upon our domestic politics, just as Greece and Rome were demoralised by their contact with Asia?" Not merely is the reaction possible, it is inevitable. As the despotic portion of our Empire, has grown in area, a large number of men, trained in the temper and methods of autocracy, as soldiers and civil officials in our Crown Colonies, Protectorates and Indian Empire, reinforced by numbers of merchants, planters, engineers, and overseers, whose lives have been those of a superior caste living an artificial life removed from all the healthy restraints of ordinary European Society, have returned to this country, bringing back the characters, sentiments and ideas imposed by this foreign environment.

It is a little hard on the I.C.S. that they should be foreigners here, and then, when they return to their native land, find that they have become foreigners there by the corrupting influences with which they are surrounded here. We import them as raw material to our own disadvantage, and when we export them as manufactured here, Great Britain and India alike suffer from their reactionary tendencies. The results are unsatisfactory to both sides.

The First Test Applied

Let us now apply Gokhale's first test. What has the Bureaucracy done for "education, sanitation, agricultural improvement, and so forth"? I must put the facts very briefly, but they are indisputable.

Education. The percentage to the whole population of children receiving education is 2.8, the percentage having risen by 0.9 since Mr. Gokhale moved his Education Bill six years ago. The percentage of children of school-going age attending school is 18.7. In 1913 the Government of India put the number of pupils at 4-1/2 millions; this has been accomplished in 63 years, reckoning from Sir Charles Wood's Educational Despatch in 1854, which led to the formation of the Education Department. In 1870 an Education Act was passed in Great Britain, the condition of Education in England then much resembling our present position; grants-in-aid in England had been given since 1833, chiefly to Church Schools. Between 1870 and 1881 free and compulsory education was established, and in 12 years the attendance rose from 43.3 to nearly 100 per cent. There are now 6,000,000 children in the schools of England and Wales out of a population of 40 millions. Japan, before 1872, had a proportion of 28 per cent. of children of school-going age in school, nearly 10 over our present proportion; in 24 years the percentage was raised to 92, and in 28 years education was free and compulsory. In Baroda education is free and largely compulsory and the percentage of boys is 100 per cent. Travancore has 81.1 per cent. of boys and 33.2 of girls. Mysore has 45.8 of boys and 9.7 of girls. Baroda spends an. 6-6 per head on school-going children, British India one anna. Expenditure on education advanced between 1882 and 1907 by 57 lakhs. Land-revenue had increased by 8 crores, military expenditure by 13 crores, civil by 8 crores, and capital outlay on railways was 15 crores. (I am quoting G.K. Gokhale's figures.) He ironically calculated that, if the population did not increase, every boy would be in school 115 years hence, and every girl in 665 years. Brother Delegates, we hope to do it more quickly under Home Rule. I submit that in Education the Bureaucracy is inefficient.

Sanitation and Medical Relief. The prevalence of plague, cholera, and above all malaria, shows the lack of sanitation alike in town and country. This lack is one of the causes contributing to the low average life-period in India—23.5 years. In England the life-period is 40 years, in New Zealand 60. The chief difficulty in the way of the treatment of disease is the encouragement of the foreign system of medicine, especially in rural parts, and the withholding of grants from the indigenous. Government Hospitals, Government Dispensaries, Government doctors, must all be on the foreign system. Ayurvaidic and Unani medicines, Hospitals, Dispensaries, Physicians, are unrecognised, and to "cover" the latter is "infamous" conduct. Travancore gives grants-in-aid to 72 Vaidyashalas, at which 143,505 patients—22,000 more than in allopathic institutions—were treated in

1914-15 (the Report issued in 1917). Our Government cannot grapple with the medical needs of the people, yet will not allow the people's money to be spent on the systems they prefer. Under Home Rule the indigenous and the foreign systems will be treated with impartiality. I grant that the allopathic doctors do their utmost to supply the need, and show great self-sacrifice, but the need is too vast and the numbers too few. Efficiency on their own lines in this matter is therefore impossible for our bureaucratic Government; their fault lies in excluding the indigenous systems, which they have not condescended to examine before rejecting them. The result is that in sanitation and medical relief the Bureaucracy is inefficient.

Agricultural Development. The census of 1911 gives the agricultural population at 218.3 millions. Its frightful poverty is a matter of common knowledge; its ever-increasing load of indebtedness has been dwelt on for at least the last thirty odd years by Sir Dinshaw E. Wacha. Yet the increasing debt is accompanied with increasing taxation, land revenue having risen, as just stated, in 25 years, by 8 crores—80,000,000—of rupees. In addition to this there are local cesses, salt tax, etc. The salt tax, which presses most hardly on the very poor, was raised in the last budget by Rs. 9 millions. The inevitable result of this poverty is malnutrition, resulting in low vitality, lack of resistance to disease, short life-period, huge infantile mortality. Gopal Krishna Gokhale, no mischievous agitator, repeated in 1905 the figures; often quoted:

Forty millions of people, according to one great Anglo-Indian authority—Sir William Hunter—pass through life with only one meal a day. According to another authority—Sir Charles Elliot—70 millions of people in India do not know what it is to have their hunger fully satisfied even once in the whole course of the year. The poverty of the people of India, thus considered by itself, is truly appalling. And if this is the state of things after a hundred years of your rule, you cannot claim that your principal aim in India has been the promotion of the interests of the Indian people.

It is sometimes said: "Why harp on these figures? We know them." Our answer is that the fact is ever harping in the stomach of the people, and while it continues we cannot cease to draw attention to it. And Gokhale urged that "even this deplorable condition has been further deteriorating steadily." We have no figures on malnutrition among the peasantry, but in Madras City, among an equally poor urban population, we found that 78 per cent. of our pupils were reported, after a medical inspection, to be suffering from malnutrition. And the spareness of frame, the thinness of arms and legs, the pitiably weak grip on life, speak without words to the seeing eye. It needs an extraordinary lack of imagination not to suffer while these things are going on.

The peasants' grievances are many and have been voiced year after year by this Congress. The Forest Laws, made by legislators inappreciative of village difficulties, press hardly on them, and only in a small number of places have Forest Panchayats been established. In the few cases in which the experiment has been made the results have been good, in some cases marvellously good. The paucity of grazing grounds for their cattle, the lack of green manure to feed their impoverished lands, the absence of fencing round forests, so that the cattle stray in when feeding, are impounded, and have to be redeemed, the fines and other punishments imposed for offences ill-understood, the want of wood for fuel, for tools, for repairs, the uncertain distribution of the available water, all these troubles are discussed in villages and in local Conferences. The Arms Act oppresses them, by leaving them defenceless against wild beasts and wild men. The union of Judicial and Executive functions makes justice often inaccessible, and always costly both in money and in time. The village officials naturally care more to please the Tahsildar and the Collector than the villagers, to whom they are in no way responsible. And factions flourish, because there is always a third party to whom to resort, who may be flattered if his rank be high, bribed if it be low, whose favour can be gained in either case by cringing and by subservience and tale-bearing. As regards the condition of agriculture in India and the poverty of the agricultural population, the Bureaucracy is inefficient.

The application of Mr. Gokhale's first test to Indian handicrafts, to the strengthening of weak industries and the creation of new, to the care of waterways for traffic and of the coast transport shipping, the protection of indigo and other indigenous dyes against their German synthetic rivals, etc., would show similar answers. We are suffering now from the supineness of the Bureaucracy as regards the development of the resources of the country, by its careless indifference to the usurping by Germans of some of those resources, and even now they are pursuing a similar policy of *laissez faire* towards Japanese enterprise, which, leaning on its own Government, is taking the place of Germany in shouldering Indians out of their own natural heritage.

In all prosperous countries crafts are found side by-side with agriculture, and they lend each other mutual support. The extreme poverty of Ireland, and the loss of more than half its population by emigration, were the direct results of the destruction of its wool-industry by Great Britain, and the consequent throwing of the population entirely on the land for subsistence. A similar phenomenon has resulted here from a similar case, but on a far more widespread scale. And here, a novel and portentous change for India, "a considerable landless class is developing, which involves economic danger," as the *Imperial Gazeteer* remarks, comparing the census returns of 1891 and 1901. "The ordinary agricultural labourers are employed on the land only during the busy seasons of the year, and in slack times a few are attracted to large trade-centres for temporary work." One recalls the influx into England of Irish labourers at harvest time. Professor Radkamal Mukerji has laid stress on the older conditions of village life. He says:

The village is still almost self-sufficing, and is in itself an economic unit. The village agriculturist grows all the food necessary for the inhabitants of the village. The smith makes the plough-shares for the cultivator, and the few iron utensils required for the household. He supplies these to the people, but does not get money in return. He is recompensed by mutual services from his fellow villagers. The potter supplies him with pots, the weaver with cloth, and the oilman with oil. From the cultivator each of these artisans receives his traditional share of grain. Thus almost all the economic transactions are carried on without the use of money. To the villagers money is only a store of value, not a medium of exchange. When they happen to be rich in money, they hoard it either in coins or make ornaments made of gold and silver.

These conditions are changing in consequence of the pressure of poverty driving the villagers to the city, where they learn to substitute the competition of the town for the mutual helpfulness of the village. The difference of feeling, the change from trustfulness to suspicion, may be seen by visiting villages which are in the vicinity of a town and comparing their villagers with those who inhabit villages in purely rural areas. This economic and moral deterioration can only be checked by the re-establishment of a healthy *and interesting* village life, and this depends upon the re-establishment of the Panchayat as the unit of Government, a question which I deal with presently. Village industries would then revive and an intercommunicating network would be formed by Co-operative Societies. Mr. C.P. Ramaswami Aiyar says in his pamphlet, *Co-operative Societies and Panchayats*:

The one method by which this evil [emigration to towns] can be arrested and the economic and social standards of life of the rural people elevated is by the inauguration of healthy Panchayats in conjunction with the foundation of Co-operative institutions, which will have the effect of resuscitating village industries, and of creating organised social forces. The Indian village, when rightly reconstructed, would be an excellent foundation for well-developed co-operative industrial organisation.

Again:

The resuscitation of the village system has other bearings, not usually considered in connection with the general subject of the inauguration of the Panchayat system. One of the most important of these is the regeneration of the small industries of the land. Both in Europe and in India the decline of small industries has gone on *pari passu* with the decline of farming on a small scale. In countries like France agriculture has largely supported village industries, and small cultivators in that country have turned their attention to industry as a supplementary source of livelihood. The decline of village life in India is not only a political, but also an economic and industrial, problem. Whereas in Europe the cultural impulse has travelled from the city to the village, in India the reverse has been the case. The centre of social life in this country is the village, and not the town. Ours was essentially the cottage industry, and our artisans still work in their own huts, more

The Case for India

or less out of touch with the commercial world. Throughout the world the tendency has been of late to lay considerable emphasis on distributive and industrial co-operation based on a system of village industries and enterprise. Herein would be found the origins of the arts and crafts guilds and the Garden Cities, the idea underlying all these being to inaugurate a reign of Socialism and Co-operation, eradicating the entirely unequal distribution of wealth amongst producers and consumers. India has always been a country of small tenantry, and has thereby escaped many of the evils the western Nations have experienced owing to the concentration of wealth in a few hands. The communistic sense in our midst, and the fundamental tenets of our family life, have checked such concentration of capital. This has been the cause for the non-development of factory industries on a large scale.

The need for these changes—to which England is returning, after full experience of the miseries of life in manufacturing towns—is pressing.

Addressing an English audience, G.K. Gokhale summed up the general state of India as follows:

Your average annual income has been estimated at about £42 per head. Ours, according to official estimates, is about £2 per head, and according to non-official estimates, only a little more than £1 per head. Your imports per head are about £13: ours about 5s. per head. The total deposits in your Postal Savings Bank amount to 148 million sterling, and you have in addition in the Trustees' Savings Banks about 52 million sterling. Our Postal Savings Bank deposits, with a population seven times as large as yours, are only about 7 million sterling, and even of this a little over one-tenth is held by Europeans. Your total paid-up capital of joint-stock companies is about 1,900 million sterling. Ours is not quite 26 million sterling, and the greater part of this again is European. Four-fifths of our people are dependent upon agriculture, and agriculture has been for some time steadily deteriorating. Indian agriculturists are too poor, and are, moreover, too heavily indebted, to be able to apply any capital to land, and the result is that over the greater part of India agriculture is, as Sir James Caird pointed out more than twenty-five years ago, only a process of exhaustion of the soil. The yield per acre is steadily diminishing, being now only about 8 to 9 bushels an acre against about 30 bushels here in England.

In all the matters which come under Gokhale's first test, the Bureaucracy has been and is inefficient.

Give Indians a Chance.

All we say in the matter is: You have not succeeded in bringing education, health, prosperity, to the masses of the people. Is it not time to give Indians a chance of doing, for their own country, work similar to that which Japan and other nations have done for theirs? Surely the claim is not unreasonable. If the Anglo-Indians say that the masses are their peculiar care, and that the educated classes care not for them, but only for place and power, then we point to the Congress, to the speeches and the resolutions eloquent of their love and their knowledge. It is not their fault that they gaze on their country's poverty in helpless despair. Or let Mr. Justice Rahim answer:

As for the representation of the interests of the many scores of millions in India, if the claim be that they are better represented by European Officials than by educated Indian Officials or non-Officials, it is difficult to conceive how such reckless claim has come to be urged. The inability of English Officials to master the spoken language of India and their habits of life and modes of thought so completely divide them from the general population, that only an extremely limited few, possessed with extraordinary powers of insight, have ever been able to surmount the barriers. With the educated Indians, on the other hand, this knowledge is instinctive, and the view of religion and custom so strong in the East make their knowledge and sympathy more real than is to be seen in countries dominated by materialistic conceptions.

And it must be remembered that it is not lack of ability which has brought about bureaucratic inefficiency, for British traders and producers have done uncommonly well for themselves in India. But a Bureaucracy does not trouble itself about matters of this kind; the Russian Bureaucracy did not concern itself with the happiness of the Russian masses, but with their obedience and their paying of taxes. Bureaucracies are the same everywhere, and therefore it is the system we wage war upon, not the men; we do not want to substitute Indian

The Case for India

bureaucrats for British bureaucrats; we want to abolish Bureaucracy, Government by Civil Servants.

The Other Tests Applied.

I need not delay over the second, third, and fourth tests, for the answers *sautent aux yeux*.

The second test, Local Self-Government: Under Lord Mayo (1869-72) some attempts were made at decentralisation, called by Keene "Home Rule" (!), and his policy was followed on non-financial lines as well by Lord Ripon, who tried to infuse into what Keene calls "the germs of Home Rule" "the breath of life." Now, in 1917, an experimental and limited measure of local Home Rule is to be tried in Bengal. Though the Report of the Decentralisation Committee was published in 1909, we have not yet arrived at the universal election of non-official Chairmen. Decidedly inefficient is the Bureaucracy under test 2.

The third test, Voice in the Councils: The part played by Indian elected members in the Legislative Council, Madras, was lately described by a member as "a farce." The Supreme Legislative Council was called by one of its members "a glorified Debating Society." A table of resolutions proposed by Indian elected members, and passed or lost, was lately drawn up, and justified the caustic epithets. With regard to the Minto-Morley reforms, the Bureaucracy showed great efficiency in destroying the benefits intended by the Parliamentary Statute. But the third test shows that in giving Indians a fair voice in the Councils the Bureaucracy was inefficient.

The fourth test, the Admission of Indians to the Public Services: This is shown, by the Report of the Commission, not to need any destructive activity on the part of the Bureaucracy to prove their unwillingness to pass it, for the Report protects them in their privileged position.

We may add to Gokhale's tests one more, which will be triumphantly passed, the success of the Bureaucracy in increasing the cost of administration. The estimates for the revenue of the coming year stand at £86,199,600 sterling. The expenditure is reckoned at £85,572,100 sterling. The cost of administration stands at more than half the total revenue:

Civil Departments Salaries and Expenses   £19,323,300

Civil Miscellaneous Charges   5,283,300

Military Services   23,165,900

The reduction of the abnormal cost of government in India is of the most pressing nature, but this will never be done until we win Home Rule.

It will be seen that the Secondary Reasons for the demand for Home Rule are of the weightiest nature in themselves, and show the necessity for its grant if India is to escape from a poverty which threatens to lead to National bankruptcy, as it has already led to a short life-period and a high death rate, to widespread disease, and to a growing exhaustion of the soil. That some radical change must be brought about in the condition of our masses, if a Revolution of Hunger is to be averted, is patent to all students of history, who also know the poverty of the Indian masses to-day. This economic condition is due to many causes, of which the inevitable lack of understanding by an alien Government is only one. A system of government suitable to the West was forced on the East, destroying its own democratic and communal institutions and imposing bureaucratic methods which bewildered and deteriorated a people to whom they were strange and repellent. The result is not a matter for recrimination, but for change. An inappropriate system forced on an already highly civilised people was bound to fail. It has been rightly said that the poor only revolt when the misery they are enduring is greater than the dangers of revolt. We need Home Rule to stop the daily suffering of our millions from the diminishing yield of the soil and the decay of village industries.

CPSIA information can be obtained
at www.ICGtesting.com
Printed in the USA
BVHW08071726042Z
663000BV00018B/991